David Hough Ela

Genealogy of the Ela Family

Descendants of Israel Ela of Haverhill

David Hough Ela

Genealogy of the Ela Family
Descendants of Israel Ela of Haverhill

ISBN/EAN: 9783337092009

Printed in Europe, USA, Canada, Australia, Japan

Cover: Foto ©Andreas Hilbeck / pixelio.de

More available books at **www.hansebooks.com**

GENEALOGY

OF THE

ELA FAMILY,

DESCENDANTS

OF

ISRAEL ELA,

OF

HAVERHILL, MASS.

COMPILED BY

REV. DAVID HOUGH ELA. D. D.

ELWOOD S. ELA, PRINTER,
Manchester, Conn.
1896

PREFACE.

Doubtless this Genealogy of the ELA family would be incomplete without an acknowledgment of its incompleteness. I hasten therefore to say that after more than thirty years, during which the materials have been accumulating, I am yet unable to fill all the gaps in the family records. Doubtless also many errors will be found in the dates and names and many facts will be found wanting which should have been recorded. I can only plead the limitations of human nature and assure the kindred, near and distant, that diligent use has been made of all available information. I desire to make acknowledgment of my obligation to ELAS who have aided me in the preparation of the work and interested themselves in securing its publication. Especial acknowledgment is due to Mrs. Emily C. Ela of Rochester, Wis., Richard Ela of Cambridge, Mass., Alfred Ela of Boston, and to James H. Ela of Manchester, N. H. I shall be very greatly obliged to any who will take the trouble to send me any additional information or corrections of any errors discovered.   D. H. ELA,

Hudson Mass., (or 38 Broomfield St., Boston, Mass.)
August, 1896.

INTRODUCTION.

The name ELA first appears in the records of the town of Haverhill, Mass., in 1656, and has been continued in that town till this day. Of the origin of the name and family earlier than above stated, no trace has thus far been discovered. I have been unable to find the name among English surnames. Inquiry through " Notes and Queries," London, has failed to bring information on the subject. The most probable supposition is that it is a corruption of Ely, a name which appears among the early immigrants into the Salem Colony—or possibly of Healy, a name quite common in the region of Amesbury, or that the three are alike forms of the Norman Elié. In the history of Dunbarton, N. H., occurs the name Paul Ela once. Elsewhere the name is Paul Healy, and his descendants spell their name Healy. A somewhat numerous Ela family in Fryeburg, Me., are descended from Joseph Healy, of Dunbarton. There is no connection between this family and that of Israel Ela, though the descendants of both lived at the same time in Conway, N. H., and both spelled their name Ela.

Richard Ela, Esq., of Washington, D. C., in a letter to this writer, suggested that the names Healy, Ely and Ela have a common origin in the French, Elié, a family which has representatives in Gen. Sir John Elley of the British army, and in the distinguished Frenchman, Elié de Beaumont. Earlier, however, than these, Ela was the Christian name of a good many Norman ladies, e. g. Ela, heiress of Salisbury, wife of William Longsword.

Whatever its origin, the Haverhill family has uniformly retained the spelling Ela through all the history of that town.

3

The only other instance of the use of the name in this country, unconnected with the Haverhill family, is in the town of East Windsor, Conn. According to the records of the family received from N. S. Osborn, a descendant, John Ela was born in Lebanon, Conn., (in the part now Columbia) about 1720, and died 1757. He married ―――― Cullom and had children, Benjamin, unmarried ; Hannah married ―――― Osborn ; Daniel, born 1751, married Mary Chapman, died 1832 ; and Jonathan married Hannah Bissel of Middlefield, Mass. These children of John wrote their name Ela, as is proved by records of deeds and other legal documents, but the later generations changed to Ely.

DANIEL ELA settled in Haverhill as early as 1656, being then married and about 23 or 24 years old. He continued to reside in Haverhill till 1698, soon after which time he removed to Boston, where he died, aged 80, December 22, 1710. His wife, Elizabeth, died in Haverhill July 7, 1698. His will, dated December 17, 1710, left his estate to his wife Eleanor.

He had a son John to whom, before his second marriage, he sold his Haverhill estate, retaining a life interest.

John married Jane ―――― and had two daughters. Elizabeth died in her infancy and Jane, born February, 1704, married, June 13, 1823, Nathaniel Doane, of Cape Cod. John having no male issue, the name is not preserved in his line.

Daniel Ela seems to have been a man of energetic, perhaps aggressive, character, and of ability and influence in the town. He accumulated a considerable property, for those times, and was frequently entrusted with office by his fellow townsmen. In 1662 and again in 1673-74 he is town committee to lay out lands. He is prosecuting attorney—perhaps we should, in modern phrase, say town-agent—in 1674-75, and also town auditor of accounts of the selectmen. In 1680 he is committee on parsonage, and also to procure an assistant for the now aged pastor. In 1699 he is moderator of town meeting. His homestead adjoined the meeting house lot and the old graveyard, now the cemetery on Water street. In 1667-68 he is a licensed inn-holder, and in 1680 is fined for illegal sale of liquor. He is once fined for swearing and using reviling speeches, and once for ill-treatment of his wife ; but none of these things prevent his serving the town in the matter of procuring a minister. His deed of homestead to his son John describes him as a tanner.

There is no positive proof that Daniel Ela was the father of Israel, but its probability is very great. First, the name is very rare, practically unknown as a surname elsewhere. It is therefore doubly improbable that two unrelated families bearing this unusual name should have been located in one town. If the name is a corruption of some other, the probability is still further increased. Their respective ages make it probable that they are father and son. Daniel is forty-four or five in 1677, when Israel is twenty-one. He also has a son, John, younger than Israel but probably older than twelve, the age then of his future wife. Israel was neighbor to Daniel, and their names appear on the same legal documents. Israel died in 1700, nearly ten years before Daniel, and neither he nor any of his five children is mentioned in Daniel's will; but neither is John nor any of his family. As it has not been possible to *prove* any relationship between Daniel and Israel, this Genealogy begins with Israel.

NOTE TO INTRODUCTION.

Mr. Alfred Ela makes the following note to Introduction, page 3 : "Being convinced that the suggested origins of our surname were each practically impossible, I made three conjectures, viz : (1) that there is a final guttural in "Ela," latent, but sufficient to preserve the "a" through centuries of mispronunciation ; (2) that this name "Elagh" was Irish ; (3) that traces of this name could be found at or near Londonderry, Ireland. Lack of space prevents giving either the reasons for the above or the results thereof other than to say that these conjectures appear to be confirmed.

"Four miles from the City of Londonderry are town lands called 'Great and Little Elagh,' whereon are ruins of a royal palace-fortress still called Elagh which antedates all certain local history and is of Cyclopean build and seemingly ' the Palace ' on Ptolemy's map of about A. D. 150. The present resident at Elagh Hall in Londonderry has given me what little information he has but much more is here accessible in the elaborate Ordnance Survey of Londonderry, made by the Royal Engineers and published officially in 1837 : the latter contains illustrations and details of topography and history and supports sundry conjectures subsidiary to those above noted.

"Suffice it here to say, without more, that there should be made a critical and careful examination of the voluminous evidence relating to the origin and history of Londonderry and its inhabitants, the indications being that our ancestors can certainly be connected therewith, though whether as kings or serfs cannot be foretold. Unwelcome to some as this origin might be, it would serve to account for the '*Irish*' in many of us ; for mental traits as well as 'names are enduring—generations come and go !' "

GENEALOGY.

1. **ISRAEL ELA**, of Haverhill, Mass., (probably son of Daniel) took the freeman's oath in 1677. He had probably been a resident for some years, if he was not born there. He married, Nov. 11, 1680, Abigail Bosworth, and died March 29, 1700. His wife died Dec. 14, 1717. He was a farmer. They had children:

   i. DANIEL, born Sep. 1, 1681, died Jan. 24, 1732-3, unmarried.
   2. ii. JOHN, born June 15,1683, married Rachel Page, died April 23, 1742. She died Nov. 6, 1730.
   3. iii. SAMUEL, born Jan. 17, 1685, married Hannah Clark.
   iv. ABIGAIL, born July 27, 1688, died 1757, unmarried.
   v. MARTHA, born March 15, 1693.

2. **JOHN² ELA**, (Israel¹) of Haverhill, Mass., born June 15, 1683, married Rachel Page, and died April 23, 1742. Wife died Nov. 6, 1730. She was daughter of Benjamin and Mary (Whittier) Page, granddaughter of Thomas Whittier, ancestor of John G. Whittier. In 1710 he was a minute man in Col. Saltonstall's North Essex Regiment. They had children:

   4. i. JACOB, born Feb. 1, 1711-12, married Lydia Merrill, of Amesbury. Second married Widow Ednah (Little) Gale. He died May 2, 1752. She married 3d, Ebenezer Gage and died 1804.
   ii. RACHEL, born Oct. 6, 1714, died June 1, 1748.
   iii. JOHN, born Nov. 11, 1723.
   iv. MARY, born Oct. 28, 1726, died April 30, 1727.
   v. MARY, born July 26, 1729, died Sept. 15, 1729.

3. **SAMUEL² ELA** (Israel¹) of Haverhill, Mass., born Jan. 17, 1685, married Hannah Clark. They had children:

   i. MARY, born Nov. 13, 1709.
   5. ii. ISRAEL, born Oct. 9, 1711, married Terzah Ordway, of Amesbury, and died May 12, 1753.

iii. JONATHAN, born Aug. 11, 1713.

iv. MARTHA, born June 7. 1715, married Dow.

v. DANIEL, born Aug. 21, 1717, married Sarah Hannaford, residence Newburyport. No children.

vi. ABIGAIL, born Nov. 19, 1719, married Humphrey Chase Aug. 23, 1744.

vii. HANNAH, born March 13, 1721-2, married.

6. viii. SAMUEL, born February 27, 1724-5, married Mary Holman, and died 1784.

ix. TABITHA, born Jan. 20, 1726-7, married Richard Colby and had *Sarah*, born 1767 and *Ela*, born 1769.

4. JACOB[3] ELA, (John[2], Israel[1]) of Haverhill, Mass., born Feb. 1, 1711-12, married March 31, 1737-8, Lydia Merrill, of Amesbury, 2d married Nov. 1, 1738, Widow Ednah (Little Gale,) daughter of George and Ednah (Hale) Little of Haverhill, and died May 2, 1752. Wife married 3d Ebenezer Gage, and died 1804. They had children :

i. ABIGAIL, born 1737, died Sept. 1, 1743.

7. ii. JOHN, born Jan. 4, 1740-1, married Widow Ruth (Greely) Whittier, 2d married Ruth Sanders and died Aug. 27, 1787.

iii. EDNAH, born Feb. 25, 1741-2, married Benjamin Hannaford, Concord, N. H.

8. iv. JACOB, born Oct. 3, 1743, married July 28, 1768, Elizabeth Ayer, and died Nov. 28, 1815.

v. ENOCH, born June 24, 1745. Resided 1770, Sanbornton, N. H. A soldier in the revolutionary army, died in service.

vi. LYDIA, born March 3, 1747, married Oct. 26, 1775, Daniel Appleton and died May 17, 1826. They had *Daniel*, founder of the publishing house, D. Appleton & Co., New York.

vii. ALICE, born July 3, 1749, married Ebenezer Gage, son by a former marriage of her mother's third husband. She died Oct. 6, 1777.

viii. ABIGAIL, Jan. 26, 1750-1.

5. ISRAEL[3] ELA, (Samuel[2] Israel[1]) of Haverhill, born Oct. 9, 1711, married Dec. 23, 1740, Terzah Ordway, of Amesbury, and died May 22, 1753. They had children :

i. JONATHAN, born Nov. 28, 1741, died Oct. 27, 1744.

ii. HANNAH, born Aug. 13, 1743.

9. iii. JONATHAN, born Oct. 18, 1744, married Susannah Hunkins and died May 23, 1825.

iv. ELIZABETH, born Aug. 4, 1746, married Nathaniel Cheney. They had *Daniel,* born 1770, *Elizabeth* 1772, *Moses* 1776, *Hannah* 1779, *Abigail* 1781, *Nathaniel* 1785, *Israel* 1788, *Rebecca* 1790. Israel Cheney was a musical genius and his family were widely known as a concert troupe in the palmy days of the Hutchinson family.

10. v. ISRAEL, born April 12, 1748, married Betsey Colby.

11. vi. DANIEL, born February 11, 1749-50.

vii. SAMUEL, born Nov. 9, 1750.

6. SAMUEL³ ELA, (Samuel² Israel¹) born Haverhill Feb. 27, 1724-5, married April 21, 1748. Mary Holman removed to Londonderry, N. H., about 1755, died 1784. He was in the army in 1775. They had children :

i. SARAH, born Jan. 9, 1748-9, died Feb. 3, 1748-9

ii. TABITHA, born Dec. 25, 1749, married Richard Petty, Thornton, N. H.

12. iii. EDWARD, born June 13, 1752, married Hannah Colby, died 1812.

iv. MARY, born May 4, 1754, married Eliphalet Cheney, lived in Canaan, N. H.

v. CLARK, born July 14, 1756, married Fulton, had one son.

13. vi. DAVID, born Jan. 24, 1759, married Widow Nancy (Fisher) Cunningham.

vii. HANNAH, born June 9, 1761, married Jonathan Ferson and lived in Thornton, N. H.

viii. JOHN, born Nov. 5, 1763, married Sarah Ferson. One son died in infancy.

ix. LOIS, died in infancy.

7. JOHN⁴ ELA, (Jacob³ John² Israel¹) of Haverhill, born Jan. 6, 1740-1, married Jan. 24, 1765, Widow Ruth (Greely) Whittier. She died May 2, 1779. Second married June 22, 1780, Ruth Sanders. She died 1805-6. He died Aug. 27, 1787. John Ela was noted for his great size, weighing over four hundred pounds. They had children :

14. i. NATHANIEL WHITTIER, born Feb. 5, 1766, married Esther Emerson and died Feb. 21, 1843 at Dover, N. H.

15. ii. John WHITTIER, (twin), born Feb. 5, 1766, married June 5, 1801, Mehitable Dame.

iii. BENJAMIN, born Dec. 26, 1767, died Jan. 24, 1768.

iv. STEPHEN, born Dec. 23, 1768, died Jan. 18, 1769.

16. v. BENJAMIN, born Dec. 23, 1768, married Abigail Emerson and died Nov. 4, 1841.

vi. EDNAH, born Oct. 3, 1775, married Thomas Folsom, Portland, Me., had children, Hon. *George Folsom*, born May 23, 1803, of N. Y., died Rome, Italy, March 27, 1869. *Charles, Louisa* and *Clarissa*, married Baker.

8. JACOB[4] ELA (Jacob,[3] John,[2] Israel[1]) of Haverhill, born Oct. 3, 1743, married July 28, 1768, Elizabeth Ayer, daughter of Samuel and Anna (Hazen) Ayer, born June 22, 1748, died May, 1794. He was in the Colonial army and marched with his company April 19, 1775. He died Nov. 28, 1815. They had children:

17. i. JACOB, born May 10, 1769, married Lucinda Hough.
18. ii. JOSEPH, born May 14, 1771, married Sarah Emerson. He died Feb. 23, 1825.
19. iii. THEODORE, born March 29, 1773, married Sophia Ayer. 2d married Hannah Young.
20. iv. JAMES, born Jan. 24, 1776, married Sophia Spofford.
21. v. ENOCH, born Sept. 6, 1782, married Widow Mary Hart.
vi. ANN H., died Aug. 15, 1865, unmarried.
vii. ELIZABETH, married Nov. 30, 1815, Moses Walker. They had children, *Moses*, married Betsey C. George and *Ann Elizabeth*.

9. JONATHAN[4] ELA (Israel[3], Samuel,[2] Israel[1]) of Haverhill, born Oct. 18, 1744, married June 3, 1778, Susanna Hunkins. She died Aug. 24, 1826. He died May 23, 1825. He was in the army 1775. They had children.

i. SUSANNA, born March 21, 1780, married —— Carlton and died before 1824.
22. ii. JONATHAN, born July 29, 1783, married Sally Heath. He died March 18, 1850.
iii. HANNAH, born Dec. 18, 1786, married Carlton.

10. ISRAEL[4] ELA (Israel[3], Samuel[2], Israel[1],) born at Haverhill, April 12, 1748, married Betsey Colby. Settled at Hooksett, N. H. He was in the battle of Bunker Hill. They had children.

23. i. ISRAEL, born 1770, married Zebiah Martin. He died May 21, 1853.
24. ii. JONATHAN, born June 24, 1773, married Jerusha Martin. He died May 3, 1828.
25. iii. SETH, born 1776, married Rebecca Dutton. He died 1836.

26. iv. ENOS, born ——, married Betsey Martin.
27. v. JACOB, born 1784, married Rachel Dutton. He died 1853.
   vi. BETSEY, born ——, married Samuel Martin. Lived in
       Hooksett, N. H. They had children. *Rufus, Gilman,
       Jacob, Hannah, Sarah, Susan.*

11. DANIEL[4] ELA, (Israel[3], Samuel[2], Israel[1],) Born at Haver-
    hill, Feb. 11, 1749-50, married Aug. 1774, Sarah Brookens
    at Newburyport. Lived in Newburyport and was heir to
    his uncle Daniel. They had children.

   i. SALLY, born March 5, 1775, married Ober Nov. 22, 1801,
      and had children, *Sally Ela* Ober, married Thomas
      Callery, and had eight children. Ela Calley, born Oct.
      14, 1818, of Franklin Falls, N. H., was her son.
   ii. BENJAMIN, died Sept. 1796.
   iii. DANIEL, died 179-

12. EDWARD[4] ELA (Samuel[3], Samuel[2], Israel[1]) born at Haver-
    hill, June 13, 1752, married April 29, 1773, Hannah Colby,
    settled in Londonderry, N. H., and died 1812. He was
    selectman in Londonderry in 1794. They had children.

28. i. EDWARD, born 1780, married Sarah Page.   2d married
       Mary Dickey. He died Dec. 22, 1853.
29. ii. NANCY.

13. DAVID[4] ELA (Samuel[3] Samuel[2] Israel[1]) born at London-
    derry, N. H., Jan. 24, 1759, married Widow Nancy (Fisher)
    Cunningham, and settled at Londonderry. They had child-
    ren.

30. i. CLARK,   married   Waterman.
31. ii. WILLIAM, born Jan. 7, 1783, married Mary Moore.   He
        died Jan. 5, 1865.
   iii. SALLY, born June 6, 1785, married Feb. 1811, Col. Stephen
        Reynolds. She died Sep. 1860. They had children.
        Alfred, born Dec. 15, 1811. *William*, born Mar. 14,
        1814. *Eliza*, born Aug. 25, 1816, died June 14, 1844.
        Mary Ann, born July 2, 1818, married Dec. 22, 1842,
        died Mar. 25, 1861. *Stephen*, born Aug. 8, 1820, mar-
        ried Aug. 24, 1848, Sarah Sargent, Chester, N. H. *Sarah*,
        born June 2, 1822, married Nov. 6, 1850, George Moore
        and died June, 1875. *Lucy*, born Jan. 16, 1825, mar-
        ried Feb. 11, 1848, Joseph Montgomery and died June
        7, 1860. *Ellen*, born July 15, 1828, married Feb. 24,
        1859, Richard Kent.

iv. Lois, born April 6, 1788. married 1809, Dea. Richard Kent, Derry, N. H. She died Jan. 7, 1872. They had children. *Lois. Horatio*, born 1811. *Burton. Augustus. Myra. Richard*, born Aug. 3, 1825, married Ellen Reynolds (see above), settled Adrian, Mich.

v. CHARLOTTE, married James Kelly. She died 185

14. NATHANIEL WHITTIER[5] ELA, (John,[4] Jacob,[3] John,[2] Israel,[1]) born at Haverhill Feb. 5, 1766, a twin of John W. The mother preserved in her boys the name of her first husband. Married Nov. 7, 1790, Esther Emerson. He was a popular tavern keeper in Dover, N. H., where he died Feb. 22, 1843. They had children.

i. NATHANIEL, born Nov. 8, 1791, died Sept. 4, 1849.

ii. GEORGE, born July 11, 1793, married at New Durham, N. H., Dec. 12, 1839, Sarah Ann C. Hill. Was first Selectman in New Durham, 1842. No children. Died Jan. 11, 1858.

iii. SUSANNA, born June 19, 1795, died Dec. 20, 1875. Unmarried.

iv. CAROLINE, born Mar. 13, 1797, died Sept. 16, 1798.

v. CAROLINE, born Jan. 10, 1799, died Nov. 3, 1801.

vi. JOHN FERNALD, born Jan. 20, 1801, died Sept. 2, 1827.

vii. ESTHER, born Feb. 2, 1803, married May 18, 1825, Nathaniel R. Hill, Newmarket, N. H. They had children. *Esther E.*, born Mar. 17, 1826, married April 18, 1848, Oliver Tibbetts, Rochester, N. H. *Nathaniel Ela*, born Nov. 26, 1827, married Jan. 21, 1858, Caroline G. Tufts, Dover, N. H. *Daniel*, born Oct., 1830, died Dec., 1833. *Elizabeth B.*, born Jan., 1834, died Mar., 1850. *Charles Ela*, born Sept. 22, 1838, married June 20, 1860, Sarah E. Vaughn, Charlestown, Mass. *Mary Ednah*, born Dec. 15, 1843. *Susan Frances*, born July 9, 1845, died Sept. 6, 1847.

viii. CHARLES, born Dec. 26, 1804, died Nov. 16, 1807.

32. ix. BENJAMIN, born Apr. 23, 1807, married Martha L. P. Neal. He died Sept., 1875

x. RUTH, born Jan. 4, 1809, died 1875.

xi. CHARLES, born Feb. 28, 1811, married May 26, 1836, Catherine Wentworth. She died Aug. 1, 1836. He is supposed to have died in Texas, June, 1838.

15. JOHN WHITTIER[5] ELA, (John,[4] Jacob,[3] John,[2] Israel,[1]) born at Haverhill, Feb. 5, 1766, twin of No. 14, married Jan. 7, 1793, Mehitable Dame, Durham, N. H., where h. settled and died June 15, 1801. They had children.

    i.   EDNAH, born Aug. 13, 1793, married Daniel Cram, second married Richard Furber.

33. ii.   JOSEPH, born July 20, 1797, married Sallie Moulton.

   iii.   JOHN, born Mar. 13, 1800, died Nov. 24, 1802.

16. BENJAMIN[5] ELA, (John,[4] Jacob,[3] John,[2] Israel,[1]) born at Haverhill, Dec. 23, 1768, married Dec. 22, 1796, Abigail Emerson. Settled in Lebanon, N. H. She died Mar. 22, 1836. He died Nov. 4, 1841. They had children.

    i.   SUSAN S., born Dec. 12, 1797, married Sept. 28, 1825, Benjamin Gallup, M. D., Lebanon, and had *Benjamin Ela*, born July 12, 1826, married Sept. 6, 1859, Delia Hubbard, Rochester, Wis. *William P.*, born Dec. 9, 1828. *George H.*, born Sept. 10, 1832. *Abbie E.*, born May 4, 1835. *Edward P.*, born Sept. 16, 1837.

   ii.   ABIGAIL E., born Jan. 24, 1800.

34. iii.   JOHN, born July 6, 1802, married Julia Demarry.

   iv.   GEORGE, born June 17, 1805, married Oct., 1832, Mary N. Hazeltine, Bedford, N. H.: she died April, 1868. Second married Oct. 28, 1870, Caroline E. Hazeltine, Chicago, Ill. He died at Barrington, Ill., Dec. 12, 1882. In 1835 he settled in Cook County, Ill., in the township afterwards named for him. He held the offices of postmaster, justice of the peace and representative in the Legislature. An able business man.

35. v.   WILLIAM STICKNEY, born June 19, 1807, married Louisa R. Greenough, second married, Elizabeth Kendrick.

36. vi.   BENJAMIN, born Aug. 4, 1809, married Angeline McConahie and died April 30, 1881.

37. vii.   RICHARD EMERSON, born May 5, 1812, married Nancy E. Hubbard, second married Nancy J. Royce, third married Widow Emily Huntington.

17. JACOB[5] ELA, (Jacob,[4] Jacob,[3] John,[2] Israel,[1]) born at Haverhill May 10, 1769, married Lucinda Hough, (daughter of Hon. David and Abigail Huntington Hough, Lebanon, Conn.,) born at Bozrah, Conn., Oct. 29, 1775, and died at Lisbon, N. H., Nov., 1854. David Hough was a native of Bozrah, and Abigail Huntington of Norwich, Conn. He was in the colonial service on Lake Champlain during Arnold's expedition and afterwards settled in Lebanon and represented New Hampshire in Congress, 1803-1807. Jacob Ela settled in Lebanon, was a shoemaker and held town offices. He died April 19, 1848. They had children.

i. ELIZABETH, born Oct. 23, 1794, died at Lisbon, N. H.,
     May 12, 1877.

38. ii. DANIEL, born Oct. 1, 1796, married Sarah Plummer. He
     died Nov. 1, 1882.

39. iii. CYRUS, born Aug. 25, 1798, married Elizabeth Ela and
     died July 29, 1881.

40. iv. THEODORE, born Dec. 23, 1801, married Priscilla Wood-
     ward and died Feb. 5, 1874.

41. v. DAVID HOUGH, born July 5, 1804, married Eliza Hall,
     second married Martha A. Hall and died Nov. 4, 1846.

vi. ABIGAIL H., born Dec. 30, 1808, married Sept., 1848,
     Isaac Cross, settled in North Dana, Mass., and died
     Feb. 24, 1884.

vii. LUCINDA A., born July 26, 1814, married June 17, 1834,
     Rev. Ralph Whitney, and settled in Quincy, Ill. He
     died March 7, 1837. Second married, Oct. 22, 1838,
     Rev. John Atkinson. Settled in Bardstown, Ky., where
     they established a young ladies' seminary, and where
     she died March 15, 1863, in the midst of the armies
     of the civil war. Her children were *Ralph Whitney*,
     died in infancy. *Sarah Atkinson*, born Nov. 8, 1839,
     Westford, Ky., married Oct. 8, 1863, Richard Winans,
     M. D., U. S. surgeon, settled in Benton Harbor, Mich.
     (Her children, Charles A., 1866, Edward C., 1869.)
     Mary Atkinson, born at Bardstown, Ky., Nov. 13,
     1844, married at Toronto, Ont., April 21, 1864, Eleazer
     B. Newcomb. (Children, David B., 1865, Mary E.,
     1869.) *Charles T. Atkinson*, A. B. Toronto University,
     born Dec. 8, 1846, married Sept., 1870, Odessa C.
     Robinson. (Children, Alma A., 1871, Florine, 1876,
     Allen R., 1883, Stella and Estelle died in infancy.)

18. JOSEPH[5] ELA, (Jacob,[4] Jacob,[3] John,[2] Israel,[1]) born at
     Haverhill, May 14, 1771, married Mar. 1, 1795, Sarah Emer-
     son. Settled at Portsmouth, N. H., and died Feb. 23, 1825.
     Wife died Nov. 7, 1840, aged 70. They lived for a time
     after marriage at Lebanon, N. H. They had children.

42. i. RICHARD, born Lebanon, Feb. 21, 1796, married Aug., 1844,
     Lucia King, and died Washington, D. C., Jan. 8, 1863.

ii. SARAH, born Lebanon, N. H., Dec. 21, 1797, married Apr.
     25, 1822, Robert S. Gray of Salem, Mass. Settled at
     Portsmouth, N. H. She died Mar. 27, 1883. They
     had children. *Margaret E.*, born Aug. 14, 1823, mar-
     ried Nov. 27, 1861, Albert I. Badger, Portsmouth, N. H.
     Robert B., born Oct. 6, 1825, married Sept. 2, 1862,
     Mary E. Gardner, East Greenwich, R. I., lived in San

Francisco, Cal. *Samuel*, born Jan. 23, 1828, married Sarah E. Haines. *George Ela*, born Jan. 2, 1830, died Jan. 8, 1870. *Sarah A.*, born July 2, 1832, married May. 22, 1855, Charles H. Hersey. Lives in Boston, Mass. *Susan E.*, born July 25, 1835.

39. iii. ELIZABETH, born Feb. 8, 1800, married Cyrus Ela, Lisbon. She died Nov. 22, 1867.

iv. HANNAH DUNCAN, born April 4, 1802, married May 12, 1831, (second wife) Gardner Towle, Lee, N. H. He died at Exeter, N. H., May, 1880, aged 89. She died at Tenally, N. J., June 6, 1889. They had children. *Hamilton Ela*, born June 24, 1833, married May 23, 1853, Annie Frances Wiggin, Cambridge, Mass., and died London, Eng., Sept. 2, 1886. He was graduated civil engineer, Harvard University. In a passage across the Atlantic in the Great Eastern, when in a storm she broke her rudder post and lay for days a helpless hulk on the ocean, he devised a plan by which she could be steered and saved her from wreck. (They had children. Adelaide Ela, married Maurice Lindsay, Wiesbaden, Germany; have three children. Edith Hamilton, born Jan. 30, 1860, Pola, Austria, married Apr. 6, 1880, Capt. Frederick Leo of Prussian army. Maud Annie, born Prussia June 25, 1871, married Tenally, N. J., Sept. 28, 1893, David H. Gildersleeve; one child.) *Henry Richard Towle*, born March 11, 1839, married Aug. 10, 1867, Sarah E. Parker, and died Nov. 14, 1868. Was lieutenant U. S. Revenue Service.

v. JOSEPH, born Nov. 18, 1804, merchant, died at Mobile Ala., Feb. 21, 1861, where he had resided about thirty years.

43. vi. GEORGE W., born Jan. 18, 1807, married Mary A. Lane.

vii. SUSAN S., born July 8, 1811, married Thomas Edwards, Westboro, Mass., and died July 19, 1859. Before her marriage she had for many years a prosperous young ladies' boarding school in Concord, N. H.

viii. JAMES M., born Dec., 1808, resided at Buenos Ayres, S. A., 25 years and 5 years in California, and died July 30, 1860, at Atlanta, Ga., while on a journey.

ix. THOMAS J., born Dec., 1808, died July 19, 1817.

19. THEODORE[5] ELA, (Jacob,[4] Jacob[3], John,[2] Israel,[1]) born at Haverhill, Mar. 29, 1773, married Sept. 2, 1798, Sarah Ayer, second married Hannah Young, sister of Rev. Dan Young. Settled in Lisbon, N. H. Becoming involved in debt, and to avoid imprisonment, he left the state and his family last

heard of him in New York. His widow married Samuel Gould and went to Ohio. They had children.

i. NANCY, or ANN, born 1800, married Feb. 7, 1828, Benj. Webster, Bradford, Mass. She died Feb. 2, 1890. Child, *Ann Frances*, Mar. 24, 1829, died Oct. 1852.

ii. COLUMBUS, born 1803-4, died 1820.

iii. SOPHIA, married 1825.

20. JAMES[5] ELA, (Jacob,[4] Jacob,[3] John,[2] Israel,[1]) born at Haverhill, Jan. 24, 1776, married Sept. 11, 1796, Sophia Spofford. Settled at Lebanon, N. H., where he died Nov., 1829. She died 1862. They had children.

i. ISAAC, born 1797, married Abigail Leisure, settled and died at Green Oak, Mich. One daughter, Harriet, married Milton Fields, Whitman Lake, Mich.

ii. MARY, born 1799, married 1823, William Seavey, Lebanon, N. H. She died 1879. They had children. *Mary Ann*, born March, 1824, married 1854, Eli Darling, W. Lebanon. (Children, Grace, Alice, Daniel.) *Louise*, born May, 1826, married 1853, William Durkee, W. Lebanon. (Children, Mary, Jennie, Herbert, William J., Sarah.)

iii. SARAH and twin (died in infancy), born 1800, died at 16.

iv. ANNA, born 1802, married 1826, Benjamin Preston, and died 1879, Orange, Vt. They had children. *Franklin*, born 1828. *George*, born Oct., 1830, married Louise Bixley. (Children, George, Charles, Solon and Perley.) *Sarah*, born March, 1832, died 1838. *Thomas*, born 1834, married 1864, Lonisa Elsworth. *Louisa*, born 1836, married Addison Goldsbury. (Children, Albert C., Clara B., Willie A., Fred E., Helen.) *Harriet*, born 1838, married Abner Getchell. *John*, born 1841, married Patterson. *William*, born 1844, married Nellie Chase. (Children, Winnie, William, Elmer.) *Solon*, born June, 1846. *Charles*, born Feb., 1848, married 1875, Cora Jones.

v. ADALINE, married Fish, had *Wilhelmine*.

vi. ROSALINE, born married Thomas Keele. Settled Ann Arbor, Mich., and died 1866.

vii. LOUISA, married Burnham.

44. viii. WILLIAM AYER, born March 22, 1812, married Almira Hazen, second married. He died Mar. 4, 1884.

ix. JAMES.

x. HARRIET N., married Lawson Hurlbutt, W. Glover, Vt., and died Dec., 1885.

21. ENOCH[5] ELA, (Jacob,[4] Jacob,[3] John,[2] Israel,[1]) born at Haverhill, Sept. 6, 1782, married Sept., 1813, Mary Hart. Settled in Rochester, N. H. They had children.

45. i.   JACOB HART, born July 18, 1820, married May 10, 1845, Widow Abigail (Moore) Kelley, daughter of Enoch Moore, London, N. H., second married Oct. 2, 1880, Mary Handerson, daughter of Hon. Phinehas Handerson of Keene, N. H. He died at Washington, D. C., Aug. 2, 1884.

22. JONATHAN[5] ELA, (Jonathan,[4] Israel,[3] Samuel,[2] Israel,[1]) born at Haverhill, July 29, 1783, married Sally Heath. Settled in Haverhill, and died March 18, 1850. Wife died Feb. 11, 1874 aged 83. They had children.

46. i.   ISRAEL, born Oct. 2, 1818, married Harriet J. Clough.
47. ii.   JOHN, born Mar. 21, 1821, married Nov., 1841, Caroline Heath.
iii.   SALLY, born Oct. 11, 1822, married Dec. 22, 1844, Giles Cheney.
iv.   PLUMA A., born 1824, married July 25, 1854, Bryant Sheys.

23. ISRAEL[5] ELA, (Israel,[4] Israel,[3] Samuel,[2] Israel,[1]) born at Haverhill, 1770, married Zebiah Martin, Hooksett, N. H., where he settled, and died May 21, 1853. They had children.

i.   JERUSHA, born Jan. 7, 1795-6, died in infancy.
ii.   SUSAN, born Jan. 7, 1797, married Isaac Abbot of Concord, N. H.; had thirteen children—two pairs twins.
iii.   ISRAEL, born 1799, died Oct. 18, 1849, unmarried.
iv.   LUTHER, born 1801-2, died 1812.
v.   JACOB, born 1804, married Widow Olive Rowell, and died Dec. 15, 1858. No children.
48. vi. ENOCH N., born March, 1807, married Widow Jane B. (Hall) Poor.
49. vii. JAMES P., married Arvilla Mann, and died Feb. 23, 1881.

24. JONATHAN[5] ELA, (Israel,[4] Israel,[3] Samuel,[2] Israel,[1]) born at Pelham, N. H., June 24, 1773, married Jerusha Martin, Goffstown, N. H. Settled at Conway, N. H., and died May 3, 1828. They had children.

i.   BETSEY, died in infancy.
ii.   RUTH, born Nov. 23, 1797, married Nahum Littlefield, Goffstown. Settled in Conway, N. H. Four children.

50. iii. SETH, born Mar. 31, 1801, married Caroline Clark.
iv. ABIA, born Sept. 12, 1803, married Joseph Meserve, Brown-field, Me., had three children.
v. JONATHAN, born July 26, 1806.
vi. LOUISA, born April 26, 1811.

25. SETH[5] ELA, (Israel,[4] Israel,[3] Samuel,[2] Israel,[1]) born at Goffs-town, N. H., 1776, married Rebecca Dutton. Settled in Weld, Me., 1811, and died 1836. They had children.
i. JONATHAN, died 1829, while a student in Bowdoin College.
51. ii. ROGER, born Dec. 20, 1804, married Emily M. Carlton, second married Widow Phebe Warren, and died March 25, 1859.
iii. REBECCA, married Stephen Webster; had two sons, *Levi* and *Stephen;* four daughters.
iv. EMILY, married Daniel Beede; children, *Seth E., Clara E., Hiram* and *Emily E.*
v. ELIZA, unmarried.

26. ENOS[5] ELA, (Israel,[4] Israel,[3] Samuel,[2] Israel,[1]) born at Goffs-town, N. H., married Betsey Martin. Settled in Goffstown. N. H. They had children.
52. i. DANIEL, born July 23, 1801, married Jan., 1829, Mary Hunt, Braintree, Mass.
53. ii. SAMUEL DUSTIN, born 1806, married Charlotte Edwards, 1832, second married Widow Dolly E. Haskell, 1854.
iii. RUTH, married Hazen Abbot, Concord, N. H.
iv. MARY, married Simson S. Moulton, E. And-over, N. H.
54. v. JOHN H., born 1808, married Martha J. Cleasby. He died 1866.
55. vi. LUTHER, married Mary ——.
vii. SARAH.
56. viii. ROBERT, married Mary A. Foster. He died July 8, 1852.

27. JACOB[5] ELA, (Israel,[4] Israel,[3] Samuel,[2] Israel,[1]) born at Goffstown, N. H., Jan., 1784, married Rachel Dutton, 1807. Settled in Stark, Me., and died July 27, 1853. Wife died Dec. 31, 1868. They had children.
i. SERENA, born Oct. 10, 1808, died 1870.
ii. ROBERT, born Jan. 27, 1810, married Nov. 10, 1847, died May 15, 1876.
iii. FANNY, born Nov. 8, 1811, married Nov. 22, 1831, died Feb. 19, 1841.

iv. ROSELINDA, born Nov. 12, 1814, married Jan. 27, 1843, —— Holman.

v. ROXANNA, born Nov. 5, 1817, married April 12, 1845, —— Fish, Stark, Me., died April 26, 1869.

vi. RACHEL, born Mar. 4, 1820, married Oct. 11, 1849, Asa Waugh.

58. vii. JACOB, born May 13, 1822, married June 13, 1849, Susan R. Gilman, Athens, Me.

viii. FIDELIA, born June 5, 1825.

28. EDWARD[5] ELA, (Edward,[4] Samuel,[3] Samuel,[2] Israel,[1]) born at Londonderry, N. H., March, 1780, married Dec., 1810, Sarah Page, second married 1815 Mary Dickey. She was born March 20, 1782. He settled in Londonderry, and died Dec. 22, 1853. They had children.

57. i. EDWARD P., born Jan. 6, 1812, married Nov. 30, 1843, Isabel Gregg. He died Sept. 2, 1876.

ii. SAMUEL D., born Jan. 29, 1816, died Dec. 27, 1839.

iii. MARY, born Aug. 16, 1819, died Jan. 21, 1822.

29. NANCY[5] ELA, (Edward,[4] Samuel,[3] Samuel,[2] Israel,[1]) born at Londonderry, N. H. No record of her marriage, and her children took her maiden name. In later life she lived with her son in Warner, N. H. Had children.

59. i. JOHN, born at Londonderry, N. H., Sept. 10, 1796, married Amy Campbell, and died at Warner, N. H., Sept. 18, 1867.

ii. HANNAH.

30. CAPT. CLARK[5] ELA, (David,[4] Samuel,[3] Samuel,[2] Israel,[1]) born at Londonderry, N. H., May 7, 1780, married Mary Waterman. Settled in Londonderry. They had children.

60. i. WILLIAM C., born Feb. 15, 1827, married April 26, 1865, Harriet M. Shirley, second married July 21, 1869, Kesiah J. Cowdry.

ii. JOHN W., born 1824, died Dec. 25, 1826.

31. DEA. WILLIAM[5] ELA, (David,[4] Samuel,[3] Samuel,[2] Israel,[1]) born at Londonderry, N. H., Jan. 7, 1773, married Oct. 29, 1812, Mary Moore, of Derry. Settled in Derry, and died June 5, 1865. He was selectman in Derry 1828, '30 to '35 and in 1843, and representative in the State Legislature 1845-46-47. They had children.

i. MARY JANE, born Sept. 29, 1813, married Dec. 1, 1836. Amos Buck, Hampstead, N. H. They had *William Ela*, born April 8, 1838, superintendent schools, Manchester, N. H. *George M.*, born Aug. 9, 1841, died 1850. *Amos H.*, born Feb. 4, 1848, died 1869.

ii. CAROLINE, born Dec. 14, 1815, married April 9, 1835, Ebenezer Buck. Children, *Marietta A.*, born April 3, 1836, married James T. Hall, Nov. 23, 1856. (Had four children.) *Alvah W. Buck*, born March 5, 1839.

iii. GEORGE, born April 26, 1819, married Sarah Richardson, and died Sept. 12, 1868. No children. Resided in Pelham, N. H.

iv. EMELINE, born Feb. 3, 1825, married Edmund B. Mooers, May 4, 1847, Atkinson, N. H. Had children. *Mary E.*, born Feb. 24, 1850, married Adin T. Little, Nov. 30, 1869. Haverhill, Mass., second married Oliver Putnam, 1878. (Five children.)

32. BENJAMIN[6] ELA, (Nathaniel W.,[5] John,[4] Jacob,[3] John,[2] Israel,[1]) born at Dover, N. H., April 23, 1807, married Jan. 3, 1833, Martha L. P. Neal. Settled at Dover, N. H., and died Sept., 1875. They had child.

i. CAROLINE WESTON, born Aug. 18, 1834.

33. JOSEPH[6] ELA, (John W.,[5] John,[4] Jacob,[3] John,[2] Israel,[1]) born at Durham, N. H., July 20, 1798, married Sallie M. Moulton, born Nov. 22, 1813. In 1822 settled in Merideth Village, N. H. Was deputy sheriff 1826 to 1856; seven years selectman, and in the State Legislature 1840-'41. Died Feb., 1890. They had children.

i. LAURA EVELINE, born Aug. 13, 1834, married Nov. 14, 1852, Daniel S. Bedee, Merideth Village, second married Alvin Peavey. (One daughter, married James W. Home.)

ii. JOHN WHITTIER, born Sept. 26, 1837, married Nov. 14, 1861, Maria Chapman, Laconia, N. H. Second married   Captain Co. B, 15th Regiment, N. H. Vols., Union Army, 1862-3. Lawyer, Chicago, Ill.

iii. CHARLES HENRY, born Feb. 13, 1840, married Oct. 25, 1862, Mary E. Smith, Guilford, Vt. He died April 18, 1865. Resided in Merideth, N. H.

iv. EDNAH, born April 27, 1842, married George E. Gilman, Detroit, Mich. Have three children.

v. GEORGE B., born April 30, 1845, died April 14, 1846.
vi. GEORGE F., born May 18, 1847, died Sept. 10, 1848.
vii. LUELLA C., born March 16, 1850, died 1867.
viii. EDWARD F., born May 26, 1852, died March 26, 1854.

34. JOHN[6] ELA, (Benjamin,[5] John,[4] Jacob,[3] John,[2] Israel,[1]) born at Hartford, Vt., July 6, 1802, married May, 1827, Julia Demarry, and died April 6, 1879   Resided in Lebanon, N. H. They had children.

i. CYNTHIA A., born Jan. 5, 1828, married July 4, 1860, Joseph W. Jewett, Lebanon, N. H. Had children.
ii. JOHN H., born July 8, 1829, married Aug. 8, 1857. Mary Smith. Commercial traveller. Residence, Racine, Wis.
iii. GEORGE W., born Sept. 17, 1831, Lebanon, married. Died May, 1874. No children.
iv. ABBIE E., born Oct. 1833. married Dec. 13, 1876, Samuel Beane 2d, Meriden, N. H. Residence, Lebanon, N. H. No children.
v. CHARLES N., born April 22, 1836, married Sept. 25, 1879, Jennie N. Lewis. Printer, Topeka, Kansas. Served in the Union Army. No children.
vi. BENJAMIN F., born May 7, 1838. Farmer, Grantham, N. H.
vii. RICHARD E., born Aug. 2, 1841, married Dec. 20, 1871. Mary Gray,   Graduate Dartmouth College. Civil engineer, Kansas City.
viii. WILLIAM H., born Dec. 8, 1843, married Oct. 10, 1885, Mary Towle. Farmer: has been selectman. Residence, Lebanon.
ix. ALBERT B., born March 4, 1845, married 1883 Amy E. Coit. Farmer. Residence, Norwich, Vt. One child.

35. WILLIAM STICKNEY[6] ELA, (Benjamin,[5] John,[4] Jacob,[3] John,[2] Israel,[1]) born at Hartford, Vt., June 19, 1807, married Louisa R. Greenough, second married Elizabeth Kendrick. A prominent business man. President of Lebanon National Bank. Residence, Lebanon, N. H. They had children.

i. RICHARD EMERSON, born Dec. 5, 1835, died Nov. 1855.
ii. Infant son, born April, 1837, died April, 1838.

36. REV. BENJAMIN[6] ELA, (Benjamin,[5] John,[4] Jacob,[3] John,[2] Israel,[1]) born at Hartford, Vt., Aug. 4, 1809, married April,

1848, Angeline McConihie, of Merrimac, N. H. Graduated at Dartmouth College, 1831 ; Andover Theological Seminary, 1835. Settled over Congregational Church, Billerica, Mass., two years. Health failed. In literary pursuits, and publisher of Merry's Museum several years. Settled in Merrimac, N. H. Representative in Legislature 1869–70. Died April 30, 1881. They had children.

i. SAMUEL F., born Dec. 20, 1856.
ii. FRANCES ANGELINE, born Feb. 1849, married April 30, 1876, William M. West. Child, *Samuel W.*, born Nov. 28, 1877.

37. RICHARD EMERSON[6] ELA (Benjamin[5], John[4], Jacob[3], John[2], Israel[1],) born at Lebanon, N. H., May 5, 1812, married April 26, 1842, Nancy E. Hubbard, Rochester, Wisconsin. She died Oct. 18, 1842. Second married Aug. 12, 1850, Nancy J. Roys, Pultneyville, N. Y. She died Aug. 1, 1856. Third married Nov. 2, 1857, Mrs. Emily C. (Eastman) Montgomery, Elkhorn, Wis. He died Nov. 22, 1888. Residence, Rochester, Wis. Mr. Ela settled in Rochester in 1838 and began the manufacture of fanning mills to which he later added other farm implements, continuing the business till 1871. He was an honored, public spirited citizen, respected for generosity, integrity, and good judgment. They had children.

i. EMILY JANE, born Oct. 24, 1851, died March, 1854.
ii. ELLEN ABBIE, born Aug. 15, 1853. Married Feb. 4, 1874, John C. Woodworth, Minneapolis Minn. They had children. *John E.*, born Nov. 12, 1874. *Richard E.*, born Jan. 9, 1877.
iii. IDA LOUISA, born Oct. 12, 1855, educated at Hillsdale college, Wis.
iv. WILLIAM MONTGOMERY, born Oct. 27, 1858, educated Hillsdale college.
v. EDWARD G., born Jan. 30, 1860, died Sept. 7, 1860.
vi. EDITH C., born Oct. 6, 1861, died Aug. 30, 1889.
vii. MARY H., born July 20, 1867. Graduated University Wisconsin, 1890.
viii. GEORGE, born Oct. 11, 1868. Lawyer.
ix. EDWIN S., born Dec. 30, 1871.
x. EMERSON, born July 7, 1875.

38. DANIEL[6] ELA, (Jacob,[5] Jacob,[4] Jacob,[3] John,[2] Israel,[1]) born at Lebanon, N. H., Oct. 1, 1796, married September, 1822, Sarah Plummer, Gardiner, Me., born Aug. 6, 1803, and died May, 1872. He was a tanner and shoemaker. Was a Mason from 1819 till his death. Settled in Canaan, Me., Oct., 1825, and died Nov. 1, 1882. They had children.

    i.   MARY PLUMMER, born June 1, 1825, Gardiner, Me., died July 8, 1844.

    ii.   LUCINDA A., born Canaan, Me., Aug. 13, 1827, died June 12, 1867.

    iii.   SARAH D., born Aug. 17, 1831, died Nov. 10, 1857.

39. CYRUS[6] ELA, (Jacob,[5] Jacob,[4] Jacob,[3] John,[2] Israel,[1]) born at Lebanon, N. H., Aug. 25, 1798, married Elizabeth Ela, daughter of Joseph Ela, of Portsmouth, N. H., born Feb. 8, 1800 and died Nov. 22, 1867. Second married Widow Mary H. Hastings, Littleton. Farmer and lumberman. Settled at Lisbon, N. H., and died July 29, 1881. They had children.

    i.   JOSEPH, born March 17, 1828, died Sept. 21, 1851, while a student in Lawrence Scientific School, Harvard College.

    ii.   CHARLES B., born Feb. 6, 1830, married Widow Laura (Turner) Stevens. Soldier in 15th Reg. N. H. Vol., Union Army, died of wounds at Carrollton, La., 1862.

61. iii.   GEORGE P., born July 13, 1832, married F. Harriet Rowell, born Littleton, N. H. Residence, Bloomington, Ill.

    iv.   CYRUS, born Franconia, N. H., Feb. 26, 1834, died at McIndoe's Falls, Vt., (at school,) March 8, 1856.

    v.-vi.   Twin Daughters died in infancy.

    vii.   RICHARD, born Feb. 8, 1840. Soldier Company K, 8th Regt. Illinois Vols. Union Army, died of disease at Lisbon, N. H., Aug. 20, 1863.

    viii.   JACOB, born Jan. 27, 1844, married Widow Sarah T. Brand.

    ix.   JAMES H., born Nov. 1, 1845, married May 26, 1883, Jennie H. White, Lawrence, Mass. She died Jan. 24, 1887. Lawyer, Manchester, N. H.

40. THEODORE[6] ELA (Jacob,[6] Jacob,[4] Jacob,[3] John,[2] Israel,[1]) born at Lebanon, N. H., Dec. 23, 1801, married March 5, 1827, at Gardiner, Me., Priscilla Woodward, daughter of Deacon Samuel Woodward, Dresden, Me. She was born Jan. 29, 1796, died at Lowell, Mass., Sept. 12, 1871. He was a shoemaker and farmer. Settled at Canaan, Me., 1826, removed to Lowell, Mass., Nov., 1846, died Feb. 5, 1874. They had children.

i.   ELIZABETH, born Dec. 24, 1827, married at Lowell, Mass.. Feb. 23, 1847, James McCullough. He settled in Sherbrook, P. Q., and died April 18, 1855. She lived in Lowell and Lynn, Mass. Had children. *Frank*, born Concord, N. H., June 24, 1848, married Jan. 25, 1881, S. Fanny Crossman, (child Frank.) Second married Jan. 21, 1886, Lydia A. Littlefield. He died Dec. 26, 1892. *Flora*, born Feb. 7, 1851.

ii. NANCY WOODWARD, born Oct. 10, 1829, married at Louisville, Ky., Dec. 25, 1850, Rev. John W. Coleman. He settled at Decatur, Ill.,and died Feb. 17, 1869. Had children. *Theodore*, born Aug. 7, 1852, married Jan. 6. 1881, Melinda Goode, (children, Daniel Roy, Hattie. May and Fannie L.) *Lucy B.*, born June 3, 1855. *Alfred W.*, born Oct. 19, 1857, M. D. Denver, Col. Married Nov. 29, 1888, Belle West, Plattville, Col. Resides Denver, Col. *James Herbert*, born Nov. 21, 1860, married 1887, Mary E. Lundy, residence Colorado. *Harriet P.* born Oct., 1864, married Aug., 1893. Robert W. Hastie ; (two children,) *Abigail*, born April 9, 1867, died Aug. 16, 1867.

62. iii. DAVID HOUGH, born Jan. 19, 1831, married April 20, 1858, Louisa B. Sargent, Lowell, Mass.

63. iv. WALTER, born Nov. 17, 1833, married Susan E. Miller. Decatur, Ill. Second married April 23, 1863, Loney Godding, Woonsocket, R. I.

v.   MARIA, born May 18, 1836, married Aug. 1, 1860, Marcus Fullenwider, Champaign, Ill., died Fairmount, Ill., May 25, 1872. Had children. *Ralph L.*, born May 11, 1865. *Guy*, born——— *Ray*, born Sept. 26, 1870. died May, 1872.

64. vi. HORACE, born June 28, 1838, married   Rosa L.. Hoyt, Syracuse, N. Y.

41. DAVID HOUGH[6] ELA (Jacob,[5] Jacob,[4] Jacob,[3] John,[2] Israel,[1]) born at Lebanon, N. H., July 5, 1804, married Jan. 16, 1832, Eliza Hall, Boston, Mass. She died Nov. 6, 1837. Second married Nov. 11, 1841, Martha A. Hall, born Nov. 1819, died Feb. 22, 1859. He was a printer, learned his trade Windsor, Vt., settled in Boston, 1826 or 8. Published several periodicals and books, carrying on a large business. He died Nov. 4, 1846. They had children.

i.   WILLIAM HALL, born   1833, apothecary.   Soldier in
     11th Reg. Mass. Vol. Union Army.   Killed at Gettys-
     burg July, 1863, unmarried.   At the time of the riots
     connected with the return to slavery of Burns, the fug-
     itive slave, by the U. S. Commissioner, he was brutally
     attacked by soldiers of the Columbian Guard and se-
     verely injured.   Massachusetts Legislature made him a
     grant of $1500 in recognition of his loss by the injury.
ii. ELIZA LUCINDA, born   1835, died March 2, 1852.
iii. CHARLES H., born Oct. 1837, died March 8, 1838.
iv. MARTHA A., born   1843, married Nov. 24, 1859, Otis
     N. Chase, Boston.   Had children.   *Alice Gertrude,*
     Florence,   *Mabel L.,*
v.   MARY L., born   1846, married Feb. 11, 1869, John H.
     Nickelson, Boston, and died Nov. 19, 1889. Had child,
     Mary Lavina.

42. RICHARD[6] ELA, (Joseph,[5] Jacob,[4] Jacob,[3] John,[2] Israel[1],)
     born at Lebanon, N. H., Feb. 21, 1796, married Aug.
     1, 1844, Lucia King, of Saco. Me., she died June 11,
     1896. Lawyer in Durham, N. H., till 1832. Clerk in
     Treasury department, Washington, D. C.   Held, tempo-
     rarily, offices of auditor, comptroller, and acting assistant
     treasurer.   In the department till his death, Jan. 8, 1863.
     His family have resided, since 1871, in Cambridge, Mass.
     They had children.

i.   MARGARET KING, born July 29, 1845, died Aug. 9, 1876.
ii. WALTER, born Sept. 23, 1848, married Dec. 29, 1887,
     Hannah S. Lyman, Montreal, P. Q.   He graduated A.
     B. and M. D. Harvard.   Member of Massachusetts
     Medical Society and a frequent contributor to med-
     ical literature.   Resides in Cambridge, Mass.
iii. RICHARD, born Nov. 30, 1850, graduated Harvard, law-
     yer, resides in Cambridge.
iv. ALFRED, born Oct. 14, 1857.   Fire insurance, Boston,
     Mass. ; residence, Manchester, N. H.

43. GEORGE W[6] ELA, (Joseph,[5] Jacob,[4] Jacob,[3] John,[2] Israel,[1])
     born at Portsmouth, N. H., Jan. 18, 1807, married Mary A.
     Lane, who died April, 1843.   Second married Widow Geor-
     giana P. (Batchelder) Clark. He was a printer and publisher
     of newspapers, first at Dover and later of the New Hampshire
     Statesman at Concord, for many years the organ of the Whig
     party, of which party Mr. Ela, as chairman of the state com-

mittee, was for years the actual manager. In 1823 he was
appointed register of deeds and held the office several years.
His later life was passed on his extensive farm in Allenstown,
N. H., where he died Feb. 16, 1893. He had children by
first wife.

i.   ROBERT LANE, born April 17, 1838, married Feb. 15, 1871,
      Quincy, Ill., Sarah J. (Rollins) Whitcher. He served
      as Captain and Major in the 6th Reg. N. H. Vols.
      Union Army, 1861-65, was in the battles of Roanoke
      Island, Newbern and Camden, at Cedar Mountain, at
      2d Bull Run was severely wounded; was with the Ninth
      Corps in its Kentucky campaign, at the surrender of
      Vicksburg and Jackson, Miss., with Grant in the Wilder-
      ness, Spottsylvania, Cold Harbor, was wounded in the
      crater at Petersburg, was at the capture of Petersburg
      and the surrender of Lee. Graduated M. D. and sur-
      geon, Dartmouth, 1870. Residence, Newman, Stanislaus
      Co., California.

ii.   RICHARD, born Feb. 12, 1840. Lawyer. Captain Co. E,
      Third Regiment New Hampshire Volunteers, Union
      Army. Was at Beaufort, S. C., Fort Wagner and Ber-
      muda Hundreds. Killed in Gen. Terry's advance on
      Fort Darling, May 13, 1864. Unmarried.

44. WILLIAM AYER[6] ELA (James,[5] Jacob,[4] Jacob,[3] John,[2]
Israel,[1]) born at Hartford, Vt., March 22, 1812, married
Aug. 17, 1834, Almira Hazen. Carpenter and civil engineer.
Resided in Lowell, Mass., Emporia, Kansas, Arkansas City
and Burlington, Kan., engaged in railroad surveying, etc.
Wife died at Burlington, March 28, 1866. Second married
                 He died at Arkansas City, Kan., March 4, 1884.
They had children.

65. i.   HENRY WILLIAM, born Jan. 25, 1836. Married Lucinda
         Jones. Second married Laura J. Vaile.

ii.   EMILY S., born at Sherbrook, P. Q., Jan. 26, 1839. Grad-
      uated at Mt. Holyoke. Married April 18, 1858, Moses
      E. Grimes, Burlington, Kan. Died Dec. 15, 1858.

iii. GEORGE A., born Dec. 17, 1840. Soldier in Ninth Regi-
      ment Kansas Cavalry. Killed at Baxter Springs Oct. 6,
      1863, by Quantrell's band.

iv.   M. ELIZABETH, born at West Springfield, Mass., Jan. 21,
      1849, married Samuel Howell, died March, 1888. (Two
      children.)

45. HON. JACOB H.[6] ELA (Enoch,[5] Jacob,[4] Jacob,[3] John,[2]

Israel,[1]) born at Rochester, N. H., July 18, 1820, married May 10, 1845, widow Abigail (Moore) Kelley of Loudon, N. H. She died September, 1879. Second married October, 1880, Mary Handerson, daughter Hon. Phineas Handerson, Keene, N. H., and died at Washington, D. C., Aug. 27, 1884. He was a printer, learning his trade with his cousin, George W., with whom he was associated in publishing the New Hampshire Statesman. An early abolitionist and temperance lecturer. Was State Bank Commissioner 1855, Selectman in Rochester 1856, was in the State Legislature 1857-58, United States Marshal for New Hampshire 1861-66, Representative to Congress 1867-71, Auditor United States Treasury January, 1872, till his death. He was a very popular platform speaker. They had children.

    i.   FREDERIC P., born May 30, 1848. Lieutenant, United States Marine Service, drowned Pacific Ocean on homeward voyage from Japan in 1873.

66. ii.   WENDELL P., born Aug. 20, 1849, married Oct. 22, 1881, Lucy A. Drake, Dover, N. H. Resides at Grand Junction, Col.

    iii.   CHARLES S., born May 2, 1853, died at Denver, Col., Oct. 21, 1883.

46. ISRAEL[6] ELA (Jonathan,[5] Jonathan,[4] Israel,[3] Samuel,[2] Israel,[1]) born at Haverhill, Mass., Oct. 2, 1818, married July 1, 1841, Harriet J. Clough. She died May 14, 1876. He resided at Haverhill, Mass., and died Oct. 1, 1872. They had children.

    i.   DANIEL K., born Sept. 14, 1841, died April 11, 1863.

    ii.   EMILY E., born March 2, 1843, died May 15, 1881.

67. iii.   JAMES M., born Aug. 30, 1847, married Nov. 26, 1873, Amelia M. Hicks, Plastow, N. H.

68. iv.   ANDREW J., born Aug. 30, 1847, married Drusilla Kimball. Residence, Manchester, N. H.

47. JOHN[6] ELA (Jonathan,[5] Jonathan,[4] Israel,[3] Samuel,[2] Israel,[1]) born at Haverhill, Mass., March 21, 1821, married Nov. 7, 1841, Caroline Heath, Haverhill. He died Nov. 14, 1894. They had children.

    i.   EMELINE H., born Oct. 10, 1845, married May 31, 1864, George W. Thompson, Haverhill. Children, *Carrie J.*, born July 6, 1865, married Fred B. Fuller, Haverhill.

Adeline M., born Aug. 10, 1867, married John S. Miller, Haverhill. *Emma F.,* born Aug. 6, 1878, and *Lena M.,* born Sept. 21, 1880.

ii. ADELINE M., born March 24, 1848, married Nov. 26, 1873, Wm. L. Bickum of Haverhill. Son, *William Harold,* born July 31, 1876.

48. ENOCH N.[6] ELA, (Israel,[5] Israel,[4] Israel,[3] Samuel,[2] Israel,[1]) born at Hooksett, N. H., March, 1807, married Widow Jane B. (Hall) Poor and died Jan. 19, 1892. Resided Amoskeag, N. H. They had child.

i. JENNIE M., married Sept. 14, 1868, Harvey A. Clements, Rollinsford, N. H.

49. JAMES P.[6] ELA, (Israel,[5] Israel,[4] Israel,[3] Samuel,[2] Israel,[1]) born at Hooksett, N. H. married Arvilla Mann and died Feb. 23, 1881. She died Feb. 25, 1879. Residence Amoskeag, N. H. They had children.

69. i. SIDNEY J., born Oct. 27, 1847, married March 6, 1869, Emma Stott and died May 21, 1893.

ii. JUNIA A., married Edwin A. Tyrrell, (or Terrill) Hooksett, N. H., and died May 16, 1885. Had children, *Leona O.,* Feb. 19, 1875, *Arthur J.,* Sept. 21, 1876, *Wesley E.,* Aug. 31, 1879, *Alpha S.* and *Annie E.,* (twins) Jan. 15, 1884, died infants.

iii. WESLEY E., married Dec. 25, 1879, Martha Holt and died Sept. 28, 1883. Residence Hooksett, N. H.

iv. FLORA VIOLA, married Dec. 25, 1879, Frank Farrell. Residence, Nashua, N. H.

50. SETH[6] ELA, (Jonathan,[5] Israel,[4] Israel,[3] Samuel,[2] Israel,[1]) born at Conway, N. H., March 31, 1801, married April 20, 1834, Caroline Clark. She died June 17, 1874. Residence Conway, N. H. They had children.

70. i. CHARLES CLARK, born Dec. 27, 1834, married Sept. 22, 1860, Abby M. Perkins and died Aug. 29, 1868.

71. ii. JONATHAN C., born May 3, 1842, married Aug. 9, 1862, Sarah D. Perkins.

51. REV. ROGER[6] ELA, (Seth,[5] Israel,[4] Israel,[3] Samuel,[2] Israel[1]) born at Goffstown, N. H., Dec. 20, 1804, married March 6, 1828, Emily M. Carleton, Frankfort, Me. Both were recognized preachers in the Free Will Baptist church, when the married, and continued so through life. She died in 185 She was a great grand daughter of the "Earl of Carleton" in the seventh generation. Second married Dec. 11, 1860, Widow Phebe Warren, of Livermore, Me. He died, Fayette, Me., March 25, 1869. Residence New Sharon and Fayette, Me. They had children.

i. CYRUS STILSON, died in infancy.
ii. JONATHAN STILSON, born 1832, died 1840.
iii. EMILY, died in infancy.
iv. ROBERT DUTTON, died in infancy.
v. ROGER JEFFERSON, born May 9, 1836, married June 11, 1881, Matilda Harrison and died Nov. 20, 1893, Barnard, Vt. In Union army.
72. vi. LEVI CARLETON, born Dec. 12, 1838, married June 24, 1866, Mary A. Tucker.
vii. GUSTAVUS W., born Nov. 19, 1840, married 1860, Helen Whitney, and died, Deep River, Iowa, Aug. 23, 1863. Had son *Gustavus W.*, born, 1861 and died Kansas City, Mo., 1890. In Union army.
viii. FRANCES C., born 1841, married 1890, Hon. Charles M. Howe, Worcester, Mass.
ix. ALPHONSO E., born 1843, lives in California. In Union army.
x. EMILY ALZINA, born 1845, married 1863, Alfred Gordon. Had children, three boys and five girls. Widow. Residence, Livermore Falls, Me.
xi. ELIZABETH, born 1863.

52. DANIEL[6] ELA, (Enos,[5] Israel,[4] Israel,[3] Samuel,[2] Israel[1]) born at Goffstown, N. H., July 23, 1801, married Jan., 1829, Mary Hunt, Braintree, Mass., and died Jan. 23, 1852. She died Jan. 5, 1890. Stone cutter. Residence Quincy, Mass. They had children.

i. MARY JANE, born Feb. 23, 1831, married March 3, 1866, William Brant. Residence Hubbardston, Mass.
73. ii. JOHN QUINCY, born Sept. 4, 1833, married Nov. 30, 1852, Rosanna Nightingale. She died Aug. 30, 1868. Second married June 11, 1880, Esther A. Keyes, Boston.
74. iii. DANIEL F., born Dec. 6, 1835, married Jan. 14, 1857, Lucy Cummings. He died March 24, 1890.
iv. WILLIAM H., born April 17, 1839, died Aug. 23, 1840.
v. GEORGE W., born July 28, 1840, died March 15, 1841.
vi. MOSES P., born Nov. 28, 1843, died Aug. 1844.

53. SAMUEL DUSTIN[6] ELA, (Enos,[5] Israel,[4] Israel,[3] Samuel,[2] Israel,[1]) born at Goffstown, N. H., 1806, married 1832, Charlotte Edwards. She died Nov. 19, 1853. Second married May 7, 1854, Widow Dolly E. Haskell, Quincy, Mass. Residence Quincy, Mass., and Bowdoin, Me. They had children.

75. i. SAMUEL A., born Sept. 25, 1833, married 1858, Mary E. Nutting.

76. ii. ELISHA T. C., born 1835. married 1856, Lucy Davis, and died May 8, 1864.

iii. CHARLOTTE R., born 1837, died Sept. 5, 1840.

iv. CATHERINE, born 1840, married Sept. 17, 1857, Francis Douglass, Quincy, Mass.

54. JOHN H.[6] ELA, (Enos,[5] Israel,[4] Israel,[3] Samuel,[2] Israel[1],) born at Hooksett, N. H., 1808, married Martha J. Cleasby. Residence Hooksett, N. H. Died 1866. They had children

i. MARTHA JANE, born Feb. 1845, married July 1869, Samuel Bird, Hooksett. N. H.

ii. MARY FRANCES, married Andrew Allen, Hooksett, N. H.

iii. JOHN H., unmarried.

iv. CHARLES C., unmarried.

v. VARNUM, born March 7, 1853, married July 30, 1881, Etta J. Stearns, Manchester, N. H.

vi. LAURA ANN, married Charles H. Littlefield, Ipswich, Mass.

vii. JOSEPH R.

55. LUTHER[6] ELA, (Enos,[5] Israel,[4] Israel,[3] Samuel,[2] Israel,[1]) born at Hooksett, N. H., married 1850, Sarah J. Bryant. Residence Quincy, Mass. They had children.

i. CHARLES H., born Quincy, Mass., Oct. 4, 1853.

ii. GEORGE E., born Quincy, Mass., Sept. 17, 1855.

56. ROBERT[6] ELA, (Enos,[5] Israel,[4] Israel,[3] Samuel,[2] Israel,[1]) born at Hooksett, N. H., married at Haverhill, Mass., Mary A. Foster, of Brooklyn, N. Y., and died at Haverhill, July 8, 1852. Widow married Carter. They had children.

i. MARY FRANCES, born Derry, N. H., Feb. 23, 1845, married April 9, 1867, Frank Whittier, Haverhill, Mass., who died Dec. 1882. One son.

ii. ANN LOUISA, born at Haverhill, June 11, 1848, married Dec. 24, 1869, John H. Frink, Haverhill, Mass.

iii. GEORGE H., born Sept., 1848, died March 26, 1854.

57. EDWARD P.[6] ELA, (Edward,[5] Edward,[4] Samuel,[3] Samuel,[2] Israel,[1]) born at Londonderry, N. H., Jan. 6, 1812, married Nov. 30, 1843, Isabel Gregg. Residence Londonderry. They had children.

    i.   SAMUEL G., born Sept. 17, 1845, died July 14, 1853.

    ii. GEORGE E., born Nov. 13, 1847, married Nov. 25, 1885, Widow Elizabeth (Seward) Caverley.

· 77. iii. DAVID W., born May 3, 1849, married Feb. 7, 1883, Martha E. Lovejoy, Waterville, Me.

    iv. JOHN A., born Oct. 27, 1857, died Aug. 2, 1880.

58. JACOB[6] ELA, (Jacob,[5] Israel,[4] Israel,[3] Samuel,[2] Israel,[1]) born at Stark, Me., May 13, 1822, married June 13, 1849, Susan R. Gilman, Athens, Me. Residence New Sharon, Me. They had children.

    i.   LAURA A., born   1852, died Nov. 29, 1860.

    ii. ANNIE E., born Nov. 29, 1861.

    iii. SUSAN E., born Dec. 8, 1862.

    iv. ROSA A., born Sept. 8, 1866.

59. JOHN[6] ELA, (Nancy,[6] Edward,[4] Samuel,[3] Samuel,[2] Israel,[1]) born at Londonderry, N. H., Sept. 10, 1796, married Amy Campbell, born Feb. 7, 1798, and died Dec. 16, 1876. He died Sept. 18, 1867. Residence Warner, N. H. They had children.

    i.   BETSEY C., born May 4, 1824, married N. M. Rollins, Pittsfield, N. H.

78. ii. JOHN C., born March 3, 1826, married May 10, 1851, Clara B. Manning. Second married Feb. 28, 1853, Louisa J. Watson.

79. iii. ABNER C., born June 18, 1827, married Sabra Nute.

    iv. EMMA J., born March 16, 1837. Teacher in Manchester high school.

80. v. JAMES G., born March 27, 1846, married Aug. 13, 1867, Bettie J. Cresley.

60. WILLIAM C.[6] ELA, (Clark,[5] David,[4] Samuel,[3] Samuel,[2] Israel,[1]) born at Londonderry, N. H., Feb. 15, 1827, married April 26, 1865, Harriet M. Shirley, who died March 1, 1868. Second married July 21, 1869, Keziah J. Cowdry. He was selectman of Derry, 1858,–'59,–'62, in legislature, 1867. Residence, Derry, N. H. They had children.

    i.   MARY LUCINDA, born April 26, 1870, died Nov. 7, 1877.

    ii. EMILY MARGARET, born Nov. 12, 1871, died July, 1893.

iii. HARRIET W., born Sept. 23, 1873.
iv. WILLIAM C., born Aug. 5, 1875, died Nov. 3, 1877.
v. ROBERT S., born April 13, 1877, died Nov. 12, 1877.
vi. GEORGE E., born Nov. 12, 1878.
vii. SAMUEL, born Nov. 29, 1881.

61. GEORGE PORTER[7] ELA, (Cyrus,[6] Jacob,[5] Jacob,[4] Jacob,[3] John,[2] Israel,[1]) born at Lisbon, N. H., July 13, 1832, married April 23, 1863, F. Harriet Rowell, Littleton, N. H. Civil engineer. Residence Bloomington, Ill. They had children.

i. CLARA ELIZABETH, born Feb. 27, 1864.
ii. GUY CYRUS, born June 3, 1866.
iii. HARRIET, born July 28, 1869.

62. REV. DAVID HOUGH[7] ELA, (Theodore,[6] Jacob,[5] Jacob,[4] Jacob,[3] John,[2] Israel,[1]) born at Canaan, Me., Jan. 19, 1831, married April 20, 1858, Louisa B. Sargent, Lowell, Mass., daughter of William and Naomi (Smith) Sargent, born at Hillsboro, N. H., Nov. 27, 1832. He graduated at Wesleyan University 1857, D. D., Cornell college 1876, minister and member of the New England Southern and New England Conferences of the Methodist Episcopal church from 1858. Delegate to the General Conference of the Methodist Episcopal church, 1872 and 1884. Pastor in Providence, Lynn, Lowell, Worcester, Boston, etc. They had children.

81. i. PAUL FRANCIS, born Woonsocket, R. I., July 27, 1862, married Nov. 24, 1884, Carrie A. Aiken, Chicopee, Mass.
ii. CLARA LOUISA, born Pawtucket, R. I., April 22, 1864.
iii. EMMA TORSEY, born Providence, R. I., June 17, 1866, died April 15, 1867.
iv. ELIZABETH LYNN, born Lynn, Mass., April 7, 1871, died Sept. 27, 1874.
v. GRACE EDNAH, born Lowell, Mass., June 10, 1874.

63. REV. WALTER[7] ELA, (Theodore,[6] Jacob,[5] Jacob,[4] Jacob,[3] John,[2] Israel,[1]) born at Canaan, Me., Nov. 17, 1833, married Aug. 20, 1857, Susan E. Miller, Decatur, Ill. She died Nov. 22, 1860. Second married April 23, 1863, Loney Godding, Woonsocket, R. I. He joined the New England Southern Conference of the Methodist Episcopal church 1861, serving as pastor and presiding elder from that date. They had children.

82. i. ELWOOD STARR, born Decatur, Ill., July 2, 1859, married Dec. 21, 1882, Jennie P. Chapman, Manchester, Conn.

83. ii. EVERETT WALTER, born Norwich, Conn., Oct. 13, 1865, married April 17, 1888, Adella T. Fillmore, Worcester, Mass.

iii. SUSAN ELIZABETH, born Harwich, Mass., July 10, 1868, married April 9, 1890, Augustus L. Holmes, Fall River. Had children.

iv. FRANCES HAYWARD, born Wellfleet, Mass., Nov. 18, 1869.

v. JOHN L., born East Weymouth, Mass., June 12, 1873, died Jan. 4, 1874.

64. HORACE[7] ELA, (Theodore,[6] Jacob,[5] Jacob,[4] Jacob,[3] John,[2] Israel,[1]) born at Canaan, Me., June 28, 1838, married Sept. 17, 1861, Rose L. Hoyt, Syracuse, N. Y. Merchant. Residence Lowell, Mass. They had children.

84. i. FRED HOWLAND, born Sept. 16, 1864, married Dec. 21, 1882, Carrie M. Manahan, Lowell, Mass.

ii. GUY HOYT, born Aug. 26, 1866, died Dec. 24, 1866.

iii. HORACE ELMER, born Oct. 17, 1868. Married, Lowell, Mass., Nov. 5, 1895, Jane C. Stanley.

iv. IDA LOUISE, born July 7, 1871, died April, 1873.

v. CORA EUGENIE, born May 24, 1873.

vi. MABEL HOYT, born Jan. 19, 1876.

vii. FLORENCE WOODWARD, born Oct. 2, 1878.

65. HENRY WILLIAM[7] ELA, (William A.,[6] James,[5] Jacob,[4] Jacob,[3] John,[2] Israel,[1]) born Jan. 25, 1836, married Jan., 1868, Lucinda Jones, Burlington, Kansas. Second married Feb. 29, 1880, Laura J. Vaile. Served in Union army. Residence Burlington, Kansas. They had children.

i. EDWIN, }
ii. EDWARD, } Twins, born 1869, died

iii. CORA EMMA, born Jan. 26, 1870, married Oct. 2, 1893, George Marsh, Halls Summit, Kansas. Had son *Walter Ray*, born July 24, 1894.

iv. FRANK WILLIAM, born Oct. 6, 1873.

v. GRACE, born Jan. 1, 1881.

vi. GEORGE A., born Sept. 6, 1882.

66. WENDELL PHILLIPS[7] ELA, (Jacob H.,[6] Enoch,[5] Jacob,[4] Jacob,[3] John,[2] Israel,[1]) born at Rochester, N. H., Aug. 20, 1849, married Oct. 22, 1881, Lucy A. Drake, Dover, N. H. Residence Grand Junction, Col. They had children.

i. HELEN HAZEL, born May 11, 1883.
ii. ERLAND ORR, born Jan. 31, 1887, died Dec. 4, 1888.
iii. WENDELL DENNETT, born March 13, 1890.
iv. GWENDOLIN, born Sept. 27, 1894, died Dec. 10, 1894.

67. JAMES MUNROE[7] ELA, (Israel,[6] Jonathan,[5] Jonathan,[4] Israel,[3] Samuel,[2] Israel,[1]) born at Haverhill, Mass., Aug. 30, 1847, married Nov. 26, 1873, Amelia M. Hicks, Plaistow, N. H. Shoemaker. Residence Haverhill, Mass. They had children.

i. WILLIAM E., born Sept. 25, 1874.
ii. FRED MUNROE, born Sept. 25, 1874, died Aug. 15, 1875.
iii. ETHEL MAY, born May 17, 1878, died Jan. 12, 1888.

68. ANDREW JACKSON[7] ELA, (Israel,[6] Jonathan,[5] Jonathan,[4] Israel,[3] Samuel,[2] Israel,[1]) born at Haverhill, Mass., Aug. 30, 1847, married Drusella (or Cordelia) Kimball. Shoemaker. Residence Haverhill, Mass. They had children.

i. MAUD, born April 28, 1880.
ii. BESSIE, died 1893.

69. SIDNEY J.[7] ELA, (James P.,[6] Israel,[1] Israel,[3] Samuel,[2] Israel,[1]) born at Amoskeag, N. H., Oct. 27, 1847, married March 6, 1869, Emma Stott, of Newmarket, N. H. She died Aug. 27, 1895. He died May 20, 1893. Resided Manchester, N. H. They had children.

i. FLORA MAY, born April 11, 1870, died Oct. 17, 1874.
ii. MABEL MORTON, born Nov. 3, 1871, died July 8, 1890.

70. CHARLES CLARK[7] ELA, (Seth,[6] Jonathan,[5] Israel,[4] Israel,[3] Samuel,[2] Israel,[1]) born at Brownfield, Me., Dec. 27, 1834, married Sept. 22, 1860, Abby M. Perkins, Conway, N. H. Served in 10th Regiment Maine Vols. Union army. Physician. Died Aug. 29, 1868. Residence Conway N. H. They had children.

i. CHARLES FRED, born March 7, 1862.
ii. ANNE LAURA, born Nov. 17, 1866.

71. JONATHAN COLBY[7] ELA, (Seth,[6] Jonathan,[5] Israel,[4] Israel,[3] Samuel,[2] Israel,[1]) born at Brownfield, Me., May 3, 1842, married Aug. 9, 1862, Sarah E. Perkins, Conway, N. H. Served in 10th Regiment Maine Vols. Union Army. Residence Boston and Woburn, Mass. They had children.

i. GEORGE COLBY, born April 12, 1863.
ii. EDGAR WILLIS, born May 16, 1864.

72. LEVI CARLETON[7] ELA, (Roger,[6] Seth,[5] Israel,[4] Israel,[3] Samuel,[2] Israel,[1]) born Dec. 12, 1838, married June 24, 1866, Mary A. Tucker, Boston, Mass. She died June 14, 1894. Carpenter. Residence, Wollaston, Quincy, Mass. Mr. Ela served in Company F, 10th Regiment Iowa Infantry, Union army, in the war of the rebellion. Was in Gen. Pope's campaign against New Madrid and Island No. 10, Mo., and he first suggested cutting a canal across the bend by way of Wilson's bayou, which resulted in the surrender of Island No. 10 and the success of the campaign. They had children.

85. i   George Carleton, born Boston, May 24, 1867, married Aug. 24, 1892, Emma Louise DeForest.

    ii.   Mary Florence, born Winchester, Mass., Nov. 15, 1870.

    iii.   Louis Bertram, born Boston, Aug. 28, 1873.

    iv.   Walter Preston, born Boston Aug. 11, 1878.

    v.   Clara Louise born Quincy Feb. 26, 1885.

73. JOHN QUINCY[7] ELA, (Daniel,[6] Enos,[5] Israel,[4] Israel,[3] Samuel,[2] Israel,[1]) born at Quincy, Mass., April 4, 1833, married Nov. 30, 1852, Rosanna Nightingale. Second married, Boston June 11, 1880, Esther A. Keyes. Residence Boston, Mass. They had children.

    i.   Sarah E., born Braintree, May 11, 1853, married William Murdock. Child, *John C. Murdock*, born Sept. 15, 1876, Athol, Mass.

    ii.   Emily, born at Randolph Dec. 27, 1854, married Jan. 8, 1876, Dennis Dalrymple, Philadelphia, Pa.

    iii.   Laura, born Randolph July 31, 1860, married April, 1880, Erwin W. Doane, Orange, Mass.

    iv.   William F., born April, 1884, died Sept. 11, 1884.

74. DANIEL F.[7] ELA, (Daniel,[6] Enos,[5] Israel,[4] Israel,[3] Samuel,[2] Israel,[1]) born at Quincy, Mass., Dec. 6, 1835, married at Quincy Jan. 14, 1857, Lucy M. Cummings, of Milton. Residence Hubbardston, Mass. They had children.

    i.   Daniel, born at Quincy, Feb. 5, 1859.

    ii.   Lucy J., born at Quincy, Mass., Jan. 20, 1862.

    iii.   Eliza F., born at Quincy, Mass., March, 1865.

    iv.   William J., born at Quincy, Mass., Sept. 13, 1868.

75. SAMUEL A.[7] ELA, (Samuel D.,[6] Enos,[5] Israel,[4] Israel,[3] Samuel,[2] Israel,[1]) born   1833, married   Mary Ellen

Nutting. Stone cutter. Residence Hallowell, Me. They had children.

    i.   SAMUEL D., born at Quincy, Mass., Aug. 20, 1860, married Jennie Harris, May 6, ——— Hallowell, Me.

    ii.   GEORGE W., born Quincy, Mass., Sept. 18, 1862, died April 10, 1863.

    iii.   FREDERIC W., born Quincy, Mass., Sept. 29, 1863.

76. ELISHA T. C.[7] ELA, (Samuel D.,[6] Enos[5], Israel,[4] Israel[3], Samuel,[2] Israel,[1]) born at Quincy, Mass., 1836, married May 6, 1856, Lucy Davis, Boston. Died May 8, 1864. Residence Quincy, Mass. They had children.

    i.   WILLIAM E., born Sept. 3, 1858, married Sept., 1888, Alma E. Campbell, Penacook, N. H.

    ii.   CHARLOTTE, born Jan. 8, 1861.

77. DAVID WILLIS[7] ELA, (Edward P.,[6] Edward,[5] Edward,[4] Samuel,[3] Samuel,[2] Israel,[1]) born at Londonderry, N. H., May 3, 1849, married Feb. 7, 1883, Martha E. Lovejoy, of Waterville, Me. Residence Londonderry, N. H. They had children.

    i.   ANNA BELLE, born Feb. 25, 1884.

    ii.   EDWARD CHESTER, born Dec. 25, 1888.

    iii.   DOLLIE MILDRED, born March 4, 1895.

78. JOHN C.[7] ELA, (John,[6] Nancy,[5] Edward,[4] Samuel,[3] Samuel,[2] Israel,[1]) born at Warner, N. H., March 3, 1826, married May 10, 1851, Clara B. Manning. She died June 19. 1852. Second married Feb. 28, 1853, Residence Warner, N. H. They had children.

    i.   CLARA A., born March 10, 1852.

    ii.   FRONIA W., born Feb. 22, 1854.

    iii.   MACE T., born Aug. 21, 1856.

79. ABNER C.[7] ELA, (John,[6] Nancy,[5] Edward,[4] Samuel,[3] Samuel,[2] Israel,[1]) born at Warner, N. H., June 18, 1827, married Sabra Nute. Residence Allegheny City, Pa. They had children.

    i.   WILLIAM C.

    ii.   LYDIA N.

80. JAMES G.[7] ELA, (John,[6] Nancy,[5] Edward,[4] Samuel,[3] Samuel,[2] Israel,[1],) born at Warner, N. H., March 26, 1846, married Aug. 13, 1867, Bettie J. Cresey. Residence Manchester, N. H. They had children.

i.   Amy E., born Nov. 2, 1869, died Nov. 7, 1877.

ii.   William C., born June 17, 1880.

81. PAUL FRANCIS[8] ELA, (David H.,[7] Theodore,[6] Jacob,[5] Jacob,[4] Jacob,[3] John,[2] Israel,[1]) born at Woonsocket, R. I., July 27, 1862, married Nov. 24, 1884, Carrie A. Aiken at Chicopee Falls. A. B. Wesleyan University, 1884. M. D., Harvard University, 1894. Member of Massachusetts Medical Society. Residence Cambridge, Mass. They had child.

i.   Norris Theodore, born Cambridge, May 25, 1894.

82. ELWOOD STARR[8] ELA, (Walter,[7] Theodore,[6] Jacob,[5] Jacob,[4] Jacob,[3] John,[2] Israel,[1]) born at Decatur, Ill., July 2, 1859, married Dec. 21, 1882, Jennie P. Chapman, Manchester, Conn. Newspaper publisher and printer, Manchester, Conn. They had children.

i.   Jeannette, born March 24, 1887.

ii.   Lucy, born Sept. 4, 1891.

83. EVERETT WALTER[8] ELA, (Walter,[7] Theodore,[6] Jacob,[5] Jacob,[4] Jacob,[3] John,[2] Israel,[1]) born at Norwich, Conn., Oct. 13, 1865, married April 17, 1888, Adella T. Fillmore, Worcester, Mass. Electrician. Graduate of Worcester Polytechnic Institute. Residence Waltham, Mass. They had children.

i.   Benjamin Walter, born April 7, 1890.

ii.   Arthur Everett, born Nov. 2, 1894.

84. FRED HOWLAND[8] ELA, (Horace,[7] Theodore,[6] Jacob,[5] Jacob,[4] Jacob,[3] John,[2] Israel,[1]) born at Lowell, Mass., Sept. 16, 1864, married Dec. 21, 1882, Carrie M. Manahan, Lowell. Bank cashier. Residence Lowell, Mass. They had children.

i.   Frederic Morton, born Feb. 5, 1884.

ii.   Blanche Louise, born Nov. 20, 1886, died Jan. 17, 1887.

85. GEORGE CARLETON[8] ELA, (Levi C.,[7] Roger,[6] Seth,[5] Israel,[4] Israel,[3] Samuel,[2] Israel,[1]) born at Boston, Mass., May 24, 1867, married Aug. 24, 1892, Emma L. DeForest, born Milton, Mass., June 7, 1870. Residence Quincy, Mass. They had child.

i.   George Eben, born June 28, 1893.

INDEX OF CHRISTIAN NAMES.

INDEX OF SURNAMES OF HUSBANDS.

www.ingramcontent.com/pod-product-compliance
Lightning Source LLC
Chambersburg PA
CBHW021557270326
41931CB00009B/1258